Unmute Yourself

Speak Up to Stand Out

Nancy Medoff

Unmute Yourself

Copyright 2021 by Nancy Medoff All rights reserved.

No part of this book may be used or reproduced in any manner whatsoever without written permission from the copyright owner except in the case of brief quotations embodied in critical articles and reviews.
To request permission contact info@nancymedoff.com
The information in this book was correct at the time of publication, but the Author does not assume any liability for loss or damage caused by errors or omission.

Editor: Beth Knaus

Cover Art: Miladinka Milic

Layout: Crystal Pirri

First Edition

nancymedoff.com

Table of Contents

INTRODUCTION — 7
- Am I on mute? — 7
- The Confidence Crisis — 9
- The Million-Dollar Problem — 15

SPEAK UP — 17
- Excuse Me, I'm Speaking — 19
- Say This Not That — 29
- Find Your Tribe — 37

STAND OUT — 45
- The Rule of Three — 47
- Start with Them — 55
- So What — 61

STEP UP — 67
- Power Positioning — 69
- Negotiate Like A Ninja — 77
- Women cannot have it all — 85

THE CONFIDENCE MANIFESTO — 93
- Acknowledgements — 97
- Resources & Sources — 101

"There is no force more powerful than a woman determined to rise."
  -W.E.B. Dubois

For Ava...

They told you you are a princess.

We told you you are a queen.

You showed us all, you're the boss.

INTRODUCTION

Am I on mute?

It was a typical corporate meeting. This time, I was sitting around a board room table in Boston, looking out over the harbor with seventeen men and two other women. Throughout the meeting I was being aggressively interrupted by my colleague Ethan, and I was fuming. After the third time this happened, I finally looked around the room and declared "am I on mute?" This halted the meeting and stopped the serial offender in his tracks. The attendees were in shoch and the floor was turned over to me as the subject matter expert in the room.

Oprah talks about ah-ha moments and mine was at that boardroom table, being silenced by Ethan. I'm an extrovert, the youngest of four loud kids and in my house growing up if you didn't speak up, you weren't heard. I was awarded the Camp Chickami Screwy Screamer designation for being the most outgoing and craziest kid at camp at the age of seven. Fast forward to my career now and I'm a global keynote speaker, often referred to as fearless.

I thought to myself, if this was happening to me, what about the other women out there, the introverts and others who are afraid to speak up?

That's when I knew I had a higher purpose which is to increase the confidence of women globally so they can step into their strengths, advocate for themselves, and get that they want and deserve at work. The next step was pretty clear. I left my VP job a few weeks later and founded my company.

My mission has taken me all over the world working with women who need help advocating for themselves. From Boston to Bahrain, Sydney to Singapore, in the boardroom and the classroom I hear the same thing. Women are ready. They are tired of earning 76 cents on the dollar, they are no longer accepting sub-par projects and assignments, and they will no longer allow themselves to be silent or silenced. Our time is now.

The Confidence Crisis

In order to get where we are going, it's important to understand what got us here.

You may have heard the term "confidence gap" or "confidence crisis". This refers to women lacking confidence and how this negatively effects their career and their pocketbooks. It's not a new concept as women have been talking about this for years. Decades even. Books, videos, retreats, journals, you name it. Lots of tools and strategies have been developed for women to help overcome their lack of confidence. And guess what? It's not working.

How do I know this? Because we are still talking about it. And reading about it and YouTubeing about it. Search "female confidence quotes" and you'll get over 70 million results. Now search "male confidence quotes". Exactly. There are none. The wage gap still exists and while women have made strides in recent years, I would argue the crisis has never been worse. It's never been worse because the tide is changing, and many women are still not stepping up. They aren't raising their hand and they are still, after all these years, holding themselves back.

Research shows that confidence impacts outcomes, and that same research shows a tremendous gender gap when it comes to confidence. As recent as last year, the National Bureau of Economic Research published a paper which yet again, in the year 2020 demonstrates that women undervalue their contributions and rate themselves and their performance significantly lower than men at work. We see this anecdotally and we feel it. And so do the men.

I was having dinner with a friend of mine recently, Frank, who is a pretty successful entrepreneur. His latest business venture is a company in the healthcare industry. Blood cleaning and distribution to be exact. He has launched several successful companies, recruited numerous C-level Executives and in this case, he was looking for a CEO.

Much of the work for this company is conducted outside the United States in underdeveloped countries. He was specifically seeking a female for the role of CEO because he felt that a female would be more successful in the role due in large part to how women behave differently in the workplace. He was especially drawn to the idea that often times women are more collaborative, more inclusive, and he felt that with the sensitive nature of this work, a female would be able to gain trust more quickly. Go Frank.

During his search, he contacted former colleagues, experts in their fields, academics, and established thought leaders. He was sure that one of the women he selected would jump at the chance to lead this game changing, global company and he anticipated conducting several interviews across the globe.

After meeting with a few women Frank became frustrated by their hesitance and uncertainty. He specifically asked these women to consider the CEO role. He actively pursued them, flew to meet with them, and in many cases he had to talk them into even considering the role. The responses he received all started out the same.

Me? Are you sure? Why are you considering me? Surely, I'm not qualified? I wouldn't even begin to have all of the skills necessary to successfully lead this company. Surely you have other people who are more qualified.

Ummmmmm, WHAAAAT?

I know you can sense my disbelief as well as Frank's. If Frank had other people on his radar, he would not have pursued these women. He would not have spent hours of his time recruiting, talking to, and trying to convince these women that they would be successful in the role. He was blown away when repeatedly and consistently, each of the women he pursued could not find a way to believe in themselves and go for the position.

Here was a clear opening in the glass ceiling, that we as women continually ask for, and not one woman raised their hand and took the chance to blow through the opening. One could even argue that we have no right to ask for this type of opportunity if we keep doubting ourselves and walking away from these opportunities.

Sadly, this is the way the hiring process usually goes. Men will often apply for a position for which they are 50% qualified, while women who are equally or more qualified will only consider the position if they check off 80% of the qualifications.

Think about that. Men are applying for jobs for which they are HALF qualified. And you know what else? They're getting them.

We're not just talking about mid-level or up and coming female managers either, and Frank's is not an isolated incident. Women are self-selecting themselves out of CEO level positions because women are sidelined into non-P&L responsible roles. Why?

They aren't going for them.

A 2021 Korn Ferry study profiled 57 female CEOs, half of which never thought about a CEO role because they didn't think they had it in them. In fact, the position wasn't even on their radar until they were specifically told they would make a great CEO. And guess who told them this? The men.

How many times have you been driving along in your car, windows down, sunglasses on, blissing out to a "girl power" song? Demi Lovato, Lizzo, Queen Bey, the list goes on and on. What's wrong with being, what's wrong with being, what's wrong with being confident? I'm on the edge...of glory! Yasssss girl! We sing along, we claim our power, we high five each other all day long and then we stop short. We don't take the step. Or the leap. Or the nudge. In fact, we don't even walk through the doors which are being opened for us.

Here's the good news – confidence is a skill, and it can be learned. If you're ready to step into your authenticity, own your strengths and communicate with clarity and confidence, you've picked up the right book.

Take a minute before you settle in to access the **unmute yourself** tools at www.nancymedoff.com/unmute - because we're just getting started.

The Million-Dollar Problem

On the day this book was published, women were earning 76 cents on the dollar compared to their male colleagues, and a mere 7% of Fortune 100 CEOS are female.

Seven flipping percent.

We've made progress in recent years but make no mistake, women are still holding themselves back and not asking for what they deserve at work. Let's look at the gender wage gap and play this out over the average career lifetime. To make it easy, we can use the latest salary metric which reports the average salary of a full-time employed woman is 18% less than the average salary of a full-time employed man.

If we start in 2020, the average female will miss out on $430,480 over the course of a forty-year career. This number is based on a white female.

A woman of color will lose $877,480 over the course of the same forty-year career, while a Latina woman will lose $1,007,080 over the same period of time.

ONE MILLION DOLLARS!!

Our lack of confidence is COSTING US BIG MONEY.
Hard dollars.
Cold cash.

The quan.
Mucho dinero.

However, you need to say it, say it loud. Bonus points for saying it in the mirror to yourself before your next salary negotiation.

These statistics are shocking and infuriating, however we can't 100% blame the patriarchy here. Women's lack of confidence is clearly holding them back. One recent metric reports that on average men think they deserve 20% more in annual salary than women think they deserve.

Men ask for more, and they get it. Plain and simple. And you can get it, too.

Section 1

SPEAK UP

Chapter 1
Excuse Me, I'm Speaking

*"You teach people how to treat
you by what you allow, what you
stop and what you reinforce."*
–Tony Gaskins

Have you ever been interrupted, talked over or sidelined? This chapter offers tactics to help you overcome daily conversational aggressions both at work and at home.

Manterrupting, Hepeating, Mansplaining: every female in business has experienced at least one of the three gender based behavioral phenomena listed here. Often times this behavior is unintentional. Often times it is overt. Regardless of the intent, the person speaking over you is forcing you to be "on mute" and the outcome is the same. You become frustrated, de-motivated and in the worst case, silenced. The next time, you may not raise your hand, or share your idea or ask the question. You stop speaking up. And that is the real tragedy.

The three tactics which follow are effective for overcoming aggressive interruptions and taking back the mic.

Manterrupting

"Excuse Me, I'm Speaking" became buzz-worthy after the 2021 Vice Presidential debates. These five words are how Vice President Kamala Harris reclaimed her voice, re-centered the attention and took back the microphone during a very high stakes debate. And these five words will forever go down in history.

You'll notice when watching the brief recap <u>here on YouTube</u> that during interruption number three, Vice President Harris asserts herself with a big, beautiful smile on her face while at the same time completely shutting down her opponent. This tactic was executed flawlessly and now you can do the same when this happens to you. Just follow these three simple steps:

1. Start with a smile.

A big, wide and genuine smile is your best offense. A smile instantly disarms people and situations. You are viewed as friendly, upbeat and non-confrontational. Vice President Harris was well prepared for this and the approach served her well. You can substitute your own words here such as "one moment, or "just a second" or "insert your favorite term here". The words are not as important here as the action. Stand firm. Polite, but firm.

2. Do not, under any circumstances, take it personally.

Research shows that most people do not even realize they're interrupting, and, in many cases, they can't help themselves. They are either excited or agitated and sometimes even in agreement. They want to be heard. They may need to make a point. They may want to sound smart. They might need to prove something to themselves or to others in the room. Maybe they were just raised this way. Notice anything here? Their behavior is about THEM. Not you. If you take it personally, you make the situation about you and shift the focus to how you're behaving rather than what you're saying.

3. Politely pause.
Once. I'll be honest here - this is my least favorite tactic even though I use this frequently myself. Here's what it looks like. If I have the floor and someone keeps talking over me, I politely pause and let them go on. Sometimes I will close my mouth and take a step back. I'll often wait a few extra moments after they're done speaking. The silence is unsettling for everyone and this awkwardness ensures that the offender won't do it again. If for some reason you want to make it really awkward for the interrupter, you can take this a bit further by sitting down if you were standing. This action may sound subservient. Here I am writing a book about how to step up and I'm recommending that you sit down when someone is trying to silence you. Au contraire. This tactic is a skillful and subtle way of claiming your power. You are owning your influence by non-verbally saying "I'm

comfortable with what I have to say and if you are so desperate to be heard, by all means go ahead I can wait".

Regardless of how you pause, the people in the room will notice what's happening. They will in many cases ask you to "go on" or "keep going" and in essence take the floor back for you. The first time this happens you can just politely let the person speak. No harm here. If it happens again? Refer to tip #1 or #2.

The underlying theme in all three of these tactics is to take the high road. Be polite but firm, realize that the offending behavior is not about you, and above all else, bring the focus back to you with a smile.

<u>Hepeating</u>
This term was first made famous by astronomer and physics professor Nicole Gugliucci when she shared the term in a tweet several years ago which went viral within a few hours. To put it simply, hepeating is when you, a female surfaces an idea or suggestion which is not acted upon. Later, when this same idea is repeated by a male colleague, he is recognized and rewarded for your idea. Pretty irritating, no? Imagine how Elizabeth Magie felt when Charles Darrow presented her idea for a board game back in 1935 and published it as his own. You may have heard of the game. Monopoly.

Now that we know what to call this behavioral offense, how do we overcome this when it happens to us? The solution is simple, yet rare.

1. Amplify.
This is where women and men can support women by AMPLIFYing them. In this context, AMPLIFY means specifically and consistently acknowledge and re-share your female colleague's ideas while giving credit where credit is due. "It sounds like Bonnie's suggestion to streamline our vendor model by doing xyz would address this issue, Bob. Wouldn't you agree"? Or "That's an excellent idea Kathy, when you brought this up last week, I'm not sure we all realized the impact your idea could have on our organization". "I really like Megan's suggestion to create a program specifically for this initiative – we should get her thoughts on the next steps".

Or, your support could be as simple as "that's a great idea Beth, thanks for sharing".

2. Clarify.
You'll need courage and confidence for this next step and I recommend you practice this so you sound polished, professional and kind. "I'm glad you agree with me, Mike. Let's talk about how to implement my idea". "Thank you for clarifying my idea, Jim – you did a great job articulating my point".

The key here is sincerity and kindness. If spoken harshly or with even a hint of irritation – you run the risk of coming across strident or petty. Take the emotion out of the situation and just state the facts. With a smile of course.

3. Look inward.
If you find your ideas are being overlooked often, you also may need to take a look at how you're presenting yourself. Are you communicating with confidence? Are you clear, concise and compelling? Section Two of this book walks you through steps for presenting your ideas with clarity and confidence along with tools to help you frame your positioning statements.

Mansplaining
I would be remiss if I didn't acknowledge the timeless classic of mansplaining as part of this gender biased communication discussion. This particular behavior is the one I find the most irritating, likely because I find this happens the most. The Oxford Dictionary defines mansplaining as "the explanation of something by a man, typically to a woman, in a manner regarded as condescending or patronizing." It's important to note here that many times mansplaining is the result of someone simply over-explaining. There may be no gender bias involved and the over-explainer just likes to over-explain.

How to overcome mansplaining:

Always start with a thank you and here your smile is again the best tool in your toolbox. "Thank you so much, Chad." And leave it at that. Or, depending on the situation you could add: "I never get tired of talking about this, even after ten years of schooling on this subject". Or "Thanks, Chad. I appreciate your opinion and trust that in turn you can appreciate my correcting you. This is not, in fact true."

The key to successfully implementing any of these tactics is to do so with confidence and grace. Our Vice President Harris example could have turned out very differently had she not softened her approach with a smile the first two times she was interrupted. Had her tone been different, had she used confrontational body language and had she not softened her approach with that big, beautiful smile, she would have been railed for being too strident, a bully, bitchy, you name it. Fair? No. Reality? Yes.

A footnote about smiling:
I've led several workshops recently where women have resented being told to smile. I understand this may sound patronizing or demeaning. And I agree that men are not being told to smile. This book is about how to speak up and be heard, and how to be persuasive in your communication. The reality is that using body language which shows you are approachable works

I stand by my suggestion to smile, until the world changes and women are no longer judged differently than men.

Your Call to Action

Choose one of the gender bias conversation behaviors listed here and make a plan for how you will overcome this when it happens to you again. Be specific. Write it down in your Confidence Manifesto. Practice. Found at www.nancymedoff.com/unmute

Chapter 2
Say This Not That

Each time a woman stands up for herself, without knowing it possibly, without claiming it, she stands up for all women.
-Maya Angelou

Sorry, not sorry: say this not that to stop sabotaging yourself at work.

As women we are judged for what we say and how we say it. Is this fair? No. Is this factual? Yes. While we don't have to be happy about this – we can understand and work to overcome this gender bias. If hearing this gets you worked up, I understand.

At the same time, I'm a realist and the facts remain that words matter more for us because we are women. Let's look at Hillary Clinton and politics in general.

Over the course of her 25-year career in politics, Hillary strategically changed how she spoke or specifically, as her career progressed, she spoke in an increasingly "masculine way" in an attempt to be more compelling in her communication. She was judged for that, too, by the way.

Margaret Thatcher trained herself to lower the pitch of her voice to sound more authoritative and women in the spotlight today are still being told their voice is annoying and shrill. Ever heard this critique of a male?

Since you cannot and should not change the biology of your voice, what can you do? While I rarely advocate for a woman to "act like a man", when it comes to word choice, this is one situation where I support behaving more "like a man" in order to communicate with confidence.

This is a catch 22 and we all have seen this. Let's go back to Hillary. If she expressed emotion, she was viewed as being too emotional. When she's steadfast and strong, she's a bitch. Women are more likely to be criticized when expressing themselves which is why it's important for women to choose their words carefully.

Here's how:
Following are a few words to remove from your vocabulary immediately. We start with the big three.

Sorry (when you don't mean it) - starting a sentence with "sorry but" or "I'm sorry" or "I'm sorry if this has already been mentioned" is an unconscious habit which is prevalent with many women. It is a career confidence de-railer and the frequency at which this happens is alarming. Think about it – you are apologizing for speaking before you are speaking. You are apologizing for being.

Take a look around, start listening and you'll see how prevalent this behavior really is for women. From standing in someone's way at the grocery store, to waiting for your coffee at Starbucks, to raising your hand in a meeting and starting your sentence with "I'm sorry but". Women apologize often in situations where the apology is not warranted. Take stock in the coming days of how often you hear yourself or other women start their sentence with "I'm sorry". Yikes.

Just - First, just try to remove this word from your communication. See what I did there? First, try to remove this word from your communication. "Just" is an extra word which is not necessary and weakens your position.

You can replace:
"I'm just checking on" with "I'm checking on"
"I'm just emailing to find out" with "I'm emailing today because"
"Just wondering if you'd have the time to review" with "Have you had the time to review"

By using the word "just" you are already diminishing your statement and your point. Think about it.

31

You're apologizing for doing your job and you sound hesitant and unsure.

Please (in email) - Yes, you must remove the word "please" from your emails. I say this understanding fully that it will be highly controversial.

I had a female boss years ago who told me to stop using the word "please" in my emails. I was appalled. While I wanted to get ahead and advance my career, I didn't think I needed to be RUDE.

Please is polite. Please is collaborative. Please is a soft and effective way to ask for what you need.

Please is also never used in emails sent by men at work.

When I balked at her suggestion, she suggested I take a closer look at the emails I was receiving from my male colleagues to see how many times they used the word please. I looked through a bunch of emails and was shocked.

 Never. Not one. Ever.

I immediately stopped using please in my emails and as I did so, my leadership visibility increased.

You wouldn't use please as much in normal conversation as you do in emails. Can you imagine walking up to a colleague at the water cooler, handing him a report and saying, "Hi Mike, please see the report you asked for"?

No. You would say "Hi Matt, here's the report you asked for" or in the case of email "attached is the report you asked for".

I'm not bossy, rude or demanding when asking for something in email. I am clear, confident and polite. In fact, I will often spend a bit of time to phrase the ask nicely in lieu of using "the please". This still doesn't come naturally to me and to this day I still need to check myself.

As much as it pains you, drop the "please" in emails. The intent is commendable. The approach is not.

Other language which hurts your credibility:

Undermining phrases – self-deprecating behavior can be endearing and demonstrates humility. If you're a woman, it can also torpedo your point. "I'm not the expert here but...", "I haven't really researched this yet but..." "You may have already thought of this...". Weak, weak and weak.
How about saying "I have an idea"? It's that simple.

The humble brag - I would be remiss in discussing persuasive communication without address the humble brag. Also known as false modesty.

"Your sensible little Hyundai is way cooler than my new oversized Range Rover. You get to zip in and out of parking spots, and you have so little space, you can't take everyone's skis, poles, Yeti coolers and inner tubes when you are in Vail skiing. I envy you, I really do".

The humble brag is insincere, transparent and undermines your power.

If you have accomplished something worthy of bragging about – own it! You can communicate with confidence and humility without sounding insincere.

Here are a few examples:
"I'm so excited this project was recommended for inclusion in next year's budget. I worked hard to build the case for how this idea will help all of us to move the team forward."

"I'm flattered to have been named to the Forbes list of best-selling authors. This has been a dream of mine for years. I know I am in great company and have so many to thank for their support."

Your Call To Action

If you're feeling overwhelmed, I invite you to use this information and go slowly. Take a step back and really listen to other women. See how often you are hearing these words or phrases or even better – look at the women who don't do it.

Pick one or two phrases to start deleting from your vocabulary slowly, then you can move on to the next. Write them down in your Confidence Manifesto.

Chapter 3
Find Your Tribe

"It's better to hang out with people better than you. Pick out associates whose behavior is better than yours and you'll drive in that direction." – Warren Buffet

Find your tribe - and choose wisely.

Tribe. Posse. Mentors. Call it what you will, these are the women and men who show up for you and are relentlessly honest. Finding your tribe is harder than it sounds.

I'm not referring to your work friends who hang out with you and tell you you're awesome, build you up and like to have a good laugh. This is valuable and this is priceless. What I'm talking about is different.

What I'm referring to here is your **Personal Board of Directors.**

These are the people who care about you, know you well and will always tell you the truth, even if it's something you don't want to hear.

I'll share an example here from my own twenty-five years in corporate sales.

I was moving up the ladder at the company and had applied for a few positions for which I was not selected. I was frustrated and I considered leaving. I did not feel comfortable sharing my frustration with my boss, so I went to my Personal Board of Directors. I'll never forget when Alan, a member of my Personal Board of Directors looked at me and said point blank "Our company pre-selects for open positions which is unfortunate. I support your decision to leave." That comment hit me between the eyes for a few reasons. First, he validated what I thought was happening and that I was not getting these roles because I was not being considered in the first place. Then, his comment gave me permission and support to consider leaving, which was unheard of in my organization. Last, he was factual and unemotional, which removed the fear and anxiety out of the situation, which in turn allowed me to consider this decision objectively. I did not end up leaving at the time, and instead I made sure before applying for a position that the hiring manager was indeed considering all qualified candidates.

Think about how much time and energy this one interaction saved me. That's the power of your Personal Board of Directors.

I suggest you choose no more than six people. As you make your way through your career, people will come on and off of your Personal Board of Directors. If you're lucky, a few will be with you from day one.

They may or may not work for the same company and no more than 50% can work in your industry or for your firm or company. If you only rely on people within your company, you will only get the company viewpoint. There are a lot of smart people out there who grew up very differently than you in Corporate America, and you will benefit from an outsider's viewpoint whenever possible.

Try not to self-select people who are going to make you feel good about yourself. You need people who will be honest, who know and understand you and will help you make difficult decisions.

In the beginning these people help you to think through your options.

- When should I relocate for my career?
- Should I go for a job I won't really love?
- What's the best way to ask my boss for the promotion?
- How do I handle this difficult situation?

Later, as you grow in your career, their role will become more about validating your decisions.

Several years ago, I made the decision to leave that same company to build and lead a global sales team in an entirely new industry. I'll never forget one of my personal Board members telling me that I had been training for this new job my whole life. I knew this already, but naturally I needed to hear it from someone else.

Prepare yourself, though. They will give it to you straight. Real life examples of brutal honesty I've heard from my Personal Board of Directors is below:

"It doesn't matter why you were chosen, leverage the opportunity and go for it."

"You won't always have the answers, and you're going to need to trust yourself. If you don't, you won't succeed."
"Your reputation is everything and I've been hearing some concerning things."

"Your boss is abusive, and you aren't seeing it. You need to leave."

Sponsor versus mentor.
When we talk about mentors and those who support you at work it's important to differentiate between a mentor and a sponsor.

Both are invested in your success and both will work with you to help you grow in your career. The difference here is that **the sponsor will go out of their way to actively open doors for you**. Rather than tell you that you should go for a job, they will tell others that you should go for the job and in doing so garner support for you before you're even out of the gate. Here's an example.

My friend Diana was recently getting ready to interview for a promotion. This was a one level promotion and a really great job for her.

As she was preparing for the interview (she has been through my persuasive communications training so she was pulling together her three pillars), she got a call from a C-suite executive she knows and considers a mentor at the same company.

He was calling to share with her that he had brought her name up as a good candidate for the next next level up – an open position two levels higher than her current role and one level higher than the job she was interviewing for.

She was stunned. She considered the original promotion to be a stretch, so imagine her hesitation in considering the two-level jump? He knew she would feel and act this way and he also knew she was ready. He had gone to the hiring manager, mentioned Diana's name, shared all the reasons why she would be a great fit and in doing so, set her up to be strongly considered for this career catapulting leap.

That's a sponsor.

Your Call To Action

Think about who you'd like to serve on your Personal Board of Directors. Write down their names, brainstorm and start with ten or more people. Wait a few days and go back to that list. Edit the list down to only those you are truly excited about. Now take a look at where they work and make sure no more than 50% of this list works at your company. Next, set up a time to connect with them and ask them if they'd be willing to bounce ideas around with you from time to time and make it a point to stay connected, even when you don't need anything specific. Then commit to scheduling and keeping these calls to keep in touch regularly.

Section 2

STAND OUT

Chapter 4
The Rule of Three

"People who know what they're talking about don't need PowerPoint"
-Steve Jobs

Now that you're speaking up - it's time to stand out.

We start with the Rule of Three.

The Rule of Three is based on the adult learning principle that people remember things in threes. "Friends, Romans, Countrymen"," The Good, the Bad, the Ugly", "Snap Crackle Pop", you name it. Epic speeches, memorable advertising campaigns and famous quotes all have one thing in common – they use three words or ideas and those three words stick.

Case in point: I'll bet you recognized Snap, Crackle & Pop in the previous example and they are 90 years old! The legend of the Rice Krispie mascots has been making people smile for 8.9 decades and is still going strong. Boomers, millennials, even toddlers know & remember these three guys. And that's pretty powerful.

With this knowledge that people remember things in threes – how and where can we use this to frame our communication? Everywhere!

Job interviews, salary negotiations, presentations, business planning, discussions at home and in your community, the possibilities are endless.
The Rule of Three is also why the three-act structure is the dominant approach to screenwriting in Hollywood and why three bullet points are always more effective than two or four. Remember, it wasn't "Snap and Pop", and Nike doesn't say "Just Do" because you wouldn't have remembered those phrases.

While applying the Rule of Three may sound difficult, it's remarkably simple to execute. First you choose the three main points or pillars that you want to emphasize and then you consistently illustrate these points throughout your presentation. Or resume. Or meeting. Or interview.

Let's play this out for an interview scenario:
In chapter 7, we will create your power positioning statement, which is your headline. You can also think of this as your elevator pitch, your personal brand statement or as I like to refer to it: "why choose me". In the meantime, let's try out the Rule of Three using three qualities or strengths we often see candidates reference when they are interviewing for a job and trying to persuade the interviewer to hire them.

"Proven success in this role"

"Skilled at building relationships"

"Contagious energy"*

*This may be the first time you're hearing the phrase "contagious energy" and I encourage you to use this phrase or another unique descriptor in place of the standard "team player, optimistic or passionate". Remember, you are trying to differentiate yourself from others, so you want to stand out with the words you choose and how you use them.

Back to the interview and a question you may be asked:

"What is the one thing which has contributed the most to your success?"

Jackpot! I love when I am asked this question and you will too because you get to answer this question however you want. You are in charge.

"The one thing that has contributed the most to my success is leveraging my greatest strengths to better the team." Notice I responded with strengths, plural. Here you tactfully set the stage for not one, but three things which have contributed to your success in the role. The interviewer asked for one, and lucky them, they get three!

You can use all three of your key strengths to answer the question or pick the most relevant and use that one alone. You simply choose your approach based on your comfort level.

Point 1 - "My track record of success in this role ensures instant credibility through the organization and my colleagues really listen when I speak."

Point 2 - "I'm skilled at building relationships and as such, I create an environment where people feel comfortable speaking up."

Point 3 - "My energy is contagious which results in fast and strong support for new initiatives. "

You've just laid the foundation for three areas which you will then refer to throughout the interview, ensuring that these are how you are remembered.

Let's try this with another common interview question:

"When are you most satisfied in your job?"

For the sake of simplicity here, it's best to focus only on one of your strengths for this answer.

1 - "I'm most satisfied in my job when I can spend my time building upon the success and knowledge I've gained in my previous roles. Sharing my unique

perspective lays a solid foundation and lifts the whole team. "

2 - "I'm most satisfied in my job when I'm breaking down silos and building relationships with our business partners, so our solutions have a better probability of success."

3 - "I'm most satisfied in my job when I see my contagious energy at work in getting others as excited as I am for new initiatives. This creates a positive and energetic environment."

Here again we used each of the same three strengths and reiterated these in our answer. The end result when using the Rule of Three is that the interviewer walks away with your strengths burned into their brain. You've stated your strengths, you've proven the value of your strengths and you've demonstrated why they matter.

Boom. Don't let that mic hit you in the foot.

The Rule of Three is not exclusive to interviews. It applies to presentations, negotiations, idea pitching and any situation where you need to be persuasive. We dive deeper on the Rule of Three for presentations in the next chapter.

Your Call to Action:

Think about the top three things you'd like to be remembered for when people hear your name. Write them down. These will be your three pillars moving forward and every day, you can use one of the three pillars in your communication, until your Power Positioning Statement is flawless.

Chapter 5
Start with Them

"In order to win a man to your cause, you must first reach his heart, the great high road to his reason." – Abraham Lincoln

When positioning yourself or your ideas, a good headline is only half the battle. In order to be persuasive and successfully communicate your point, you MUST make the connection to your specific audience. You can be the most highly valued thought leader in your field, have the best track record in the world and have produced game changing results; **none of this will matter if you don't make the connection back to your audience.** You must always demonstrate the relevance of your point.

We see this persuasive communication strategy at its best with advertising campaigns. The most memorable ads focus on how the consumer will feel, or the benefits the consumer (audience) will get from the product or service. Think Volvo and safety. Coke and a smile. There is a clear distinction between a benefit (them) and the feature (you) or what you are offering.

In the two scenarios below, which is more likely to propel you to action?

Our miracle weight loss system comes with a complete menu of meals that are delicious and easy to fix.

or

Wouldn't it be great if you could eat delicious foods, spend a fraction of your time in the kitchen, enjoy a variety of dishes and still be guaranteed to lose weight?

Our ergonomically designed club head was specifically engineered to stop the over rotation that causes you to slice your drive.

or

Own the course and be the envy of your golfing buddies. With our new club, your ball will stay on the fairway, drive straight and fly further than you ever dreamed possible.

Now let's apply the "start with them" principle to you and your business or brand.

When you are making a presentation, each slide, bullet point and handout should tie back to your audience. If you don't know who is in the audience, ask. Every time I give a keynote or lead a workshop I get as much information ahead of time as possible about who is attending. What's their age? Gender? Values? Level within the organization? What are the buzz words at the company? What's on everyone's mind? What's happening in their industry or line of business?

I then use this information to tie my points back to this specific audience, their needs and their world. The content I am presenting stays the same, it's the RELEVANCE and how I tie this back to the group that will change. I'll give you an example.

I was presenting recently to a company headquartered in the Middle East, with employees working all over the globe. The topic was women Speaking Up to Stand Out and I had to understand and incorporate the fact that several different cultural norms were at play for these women. Before the session, I researched which countries the attendees were from, how many were from the Middle East versus Europe versus the United States, and what was happening with the company and their Diversity and Inclusion initiatives around women. As I was speaking, I was able to reference specific examples from Indian culture, a personal story about a recent trip to Dubai, why women in finance are still facing an uphill battle and finally how the 2020 U.S. Vice Presidential debates were a lesson to us all in overcoming aggressive interruptions. After the session I was contacted from attendees all over the world because I had connected with them and in doing so, made my point resonate with them personally. They believed in what I was telling them, due in large part because I was able to make the connection FOR THEM.

The "start with them" principle applies for one-on-one meetings as well. If your presentation is to one person, your "audience" is the person you are trying to influence. Boss, colleague, hiring manager, or a business partner – it's all the same. Figure out how what you are proposing affects THEM, then continuously make that connection out loud as you are communicating. Out loud, not in your head.

Let's say you're pitching for more staff. You need three full-time people in order for the business unit to achieve their goals. Think about what specific benefit or outcome will occur, after hiring these three people.

Morale booster for the team and for those who are already working overtime and need their personal time back?
More product? Innovation? Better quality?
Increased productivity for the team?
Reduction in errors?

Pick three (remember the rule of three) and use these three points to make a case for why everyone will benefit from these additions to the team.

Another way to approach this is to think about how easy you are making it for your audience to say yes. Yes to you, yes to your ideas, yes to your product, yes to all of it. Salespeople, like many of us often times get stuck "over selling". Listing out all of the great features of their product or service and all the reasons why their prospect should buy. In doing so, they create noise and overwhelm. I call this feature dumping.

Instead, laser in on the three biggest issues your product or service will solve for your customer and stick to only those three in order to be memorable.

And who doesn't love to be remembered?

Your Call to Action

Think about a situation coming up where you need to be persuasive. This can be personal, professional, a large group or one on one. Write out why your point of view matters to your audience. If you're using your three strengths from the last chapter, add "this matters because" to each strength to make sure you are resonating with your audience. Or, skip ahead and if you haven't already done so, download the Power Positioning Template to start framing out your statements. We will polish these up in Chapter 7. www.nancymedoff.com/unmute.

Chapter 6
So What

*"Don't tell people your plans,
show them your results."
-Unknown*

If there is one and only one tip you take away from this book – this is it.

This one communication tactic is without a doubt the most powerful skill you can master to be more persuasive. It is also the simplest. And the area where people struggle the most and in doing so, fail to influence the outcome. Two little words that will change your approach a whole darn lot.

So. What.

Simple, and yet not so simple.

When you are communicating persuasively, as you are lining up your key points and deciding which three to emphasize – ask yourself after EVERY POINT:

So what?
Why is your point relevant?
Why do they care?
Why should the company care?

I'll say it again because it's that important. For every point you are trying to make, you MUST ask yourself "so what?"

The "so what" takes your connection with the audience across the finish line and is the single most effective way to make sure your point is remembered.

"So what" can sometimes be confused with "start with them" and here's the easiest way to understand the difference and in doing so, master the "so what":

Ask yourself how this idea, point or strength has worked in the past. What was the result? How did the team, client, or company benefit from the outcome? Incremental revenue? Additional savings? Cost avoidance? Innovation? Changes in morale? Culture? **What was or will be the ultimate result?**

Then keep asking "so what" until that light bulb goes off because eventually it will, and this is the holy grail of persuasive communication.

Let's try this out with a strength I hear people use 80% of the time in the work that I do with career confidence. Bonus persuasion tip– if 80% of people are using the same strength you are using, it's time to find a new way of articulating that strength. Here we use "I'm results driven."

"So What" dry run.

"I'm results driven."
Okaaaaaaaaaaay. This is a statement. It's a good statement but it's just there. Kind of like vanilla ice cream. It's ok, it will do, but it's not really exciting. Nothing is really tied to this phrase and there's no real outcome. It's not very powerful and it's definitely not persuasive.

BETTER:
"I'm results driven and I consistently meet or exceed my goals."

A little better as here we see the impact of the strength. Here we are adding some jimmies (I'm from new England, that's what we call them) or sprinkles to the ice cream. This phrase starts to get a little traction. The eyebrow goes up and you have the interviewer's attention.

BEST:
"I'm results driven and as such, I consistently meet or exceed my goals and in doing so raise the bar for the whole team."

Now we are talking! Here you are laying out your strength, the benefit to your audience, and wrapping it all up nicely with **why that person should care.** This is the ice cream sundae. You might add "I consistently meet or exceed my goals and in doing so raise the bar for the whole team. I know you have aggressive revenue targets for this year, and I'd love to help the team achieve break-through results". Cherry. On. Top.

It's always wise to tailor the "so what" to the individual you are speaking with, and their role or priorities.

If it's Human Resources or a team leader it's a good idea to provide an outcome based on how you will better the team.

"I'm results driven and as such, I consistently meet or exceed my goals and in doing so raise the bar for the whole team. This in turn boosts morale and supports the company culture."

If it's executive leadership or finance, tie your strength back to a business result. Quantify this as much as possible. Understand what's most important to the company or business unit and make the connection to how you can help achieve these objectives.

"I'm results driven. I consistently meet or exceed my goals, and in doing so always make revenue targets for the company. This raises the bar for everyone and brings the team closer to achieving stretch targets."

If it's your boss or a potential employer, don't be afraid to make the "so what" specific. There is no harm in tying back the benefit directly to the interviewer or hiring manager.

"I'm results oriented and as such I always make my goals. This means less time you will have to spend making sure I'm staying on track, and more time for you to focus on the bigger priorities for the team."

If you approach the "so what" principle the right way, it's not only effective it can also be a lot of fun. I have had many lively team meetings where we all get to shout out "so what" until the person presenting to us is able to articulate why we should care. Fun for us, maybe not so fun for them.

Your Call to Action:

Here we add the "so what". Reference your three key points and after you list the results, write down the "So What".

Section 3

STEP UP

Chapter 7
Power Positioning

"The things you are passionate about are not random, they are your calling."
-Unknown

Now that you've learned the three principles of persuasion, the next step is to leverage this knowledge with a focus on you.

Why you?

Think about how much time you spend preparing presentations. If you're in sales, it's likely most of your day is spent pulling together pitch decks or annual business reviews. If you're an executive, you have to present results, ideas and initiatives to gain buy in several times per week. If you are newer in your career, you are being asked to complete projects and report out on results. I calculated once that I spent close to twenty hours per week working on client presentations. That's almost half the work week.

Now think about how much time you spend on thoughtfully presenting yourself. Your personal brand statement? Your unique value proposition? Your elevator pitch? Here's your opportunity to sit down and really focus on you, your brand and how you want to be perceived.

The Power Positioning Statement

Good news! I've created a template for you to capture all of the great work you've completed thus far to help clearly and concisely pull this all together. Just click here or go to **https://nancymedoff.com/unmute** and click on the Power Positioning link to access The Power Positioning Template. You can edit this electronically, or if you are old school like me, print it out and fill in the blanks.

The Power Positioning Statement pulls everything together by identifying your three key strengths at work, connecting these strengths with the benefit they will bring to your target, and finally articulating the "so what" to demonstrate the specific impact.

Here is an opportunity to think again about your three greatest strengths and make sure these are how you want to position yourself for the future. Think hard about the future you. Rather than how you've always been viewed, how do you WANT to be viewed moving forward. It's your brand and you can be whoever you want.

Back to the three traits which define who you really are. If you're struggling here, just say to yourself "I am good at" and fill in the blank. Then move on to "I am also good at" and do this one more time so that you have three strengths. If you started this in the previous calls to action, even better.

Strengths with benefits – before and after:

These are examples from true life workshops where we worked through attendee's Power Positioning Statements.

Before:
I'm a relationship builder.

After:
I am good at building relationships. This matters because I can quickly and effortlessly build trust with my clients, therefore I am able to gain buy in to new company initiatives or programs which help to drive sales.

or

I am good at building relationships. This matters because I can quickly and effortlessly build an environment of trust for the team. As a result, people on the team speak freely and are able to share new ideas and suggestions, thus raising the level of innovation.

or

I excel at building relationships which makes our employees feel valued and contributes to their self-worth. When our employees are happy and we make it a great place to work, the result is better outcomes for our customers who come back again and again.

Remember! You customize the "so what" based on the role or priorities of your audience.

Before:	After:
I'm not afraid to dig in.	I'm naturally curious which means I ask a lot of questions to quickly identify and remove obstacles. This in turn ensures flawless execution and raises the bar for our clients and our company.
I'm dedicated	I'm unwavering which means I'm committed to the cause and I care about the customer. This drives confidence in the business unit, promotes teamwork, and builds customer trust. In short, I deliver (on what)?
I'm a strategic thinker	I'm a strategic thinker which means I see solutions before others even know there's a problem. Anticipating and removing obstacles earns client trust and deepens client relationships which means more sales, more clients, better results. I am a strategic thinker which means I look at things for the short and long term. As such I'm able to anticipate rather

	than react to challenges or obstacles/trends. This makes us nimbler as an organization and, in the end, saves us money.

Your Call to Action:

Download the template, complete the statement and say this out loud to someone you trust, several times. How does this feel to you? It may feel awkward and after a few times, it should feel good. You should feel powerful. Like this is YOU. If it feels good, you've made it. If it doesn't feel right, check your strengths and make sure these are really who you are.

Chapter 8
Negotiate Like A Ninja

"A strong woman understands that the gifts such as logic, decisiveness, and strength are just as feminine as intuition and emotional connection. She values and uses all of her gifts." - Nancy Rathburn

Know your value and negotiate like a ninja.

By now you should be feeling pretty confident which is important because confident negotiators are more successful. In fact, under-confident negotiators are only successful 20% of the time!

Here we apply ninja negotiation skills for a salary increase. The tactics and skills we use here apply however to any negotiation. Landing new clients, negotiating a large purchase, being chosen for a high-profile project – the list is endless.

You've pulled together your Power Positioning Statement, you've nailed the interview and you've been offered the job! This is a critical point where what you do now could shape your future with the company, not to mention your future earnings.

You've seen the 40-year wage gap example, and now I'll give you a specific example of incremental changes and how they compound over five years.

When I was leading a large inside sales team, I asked to meet with a rockstar salesperson who in the past had never seized the opportunity for a promotion and the subsequent 3% salary increase. When I asked her why she passed up the money, for five years in a row, she responded with "it's only three percent".

I was floored. Again, WHAAAT?

She was viewing her salary increase as only 3% and she had passed on this promotion for five years in a row. Let's look at the compounded impact here in real numbers. We will use a $70,000 salary and a three percent increase. A three percent annual increase, compounded over the course of five years, means she had left $11,000 on the table.

She went for the promotion the next day.

This story demonstrates how important it is to advocate for **every last cent.** If you are just starting out, the money you accept in the early stages of your career will have a significant impact on your later earnings. If you're already at the top of your game and earning more than most, think about how many additional dollars in your pocket just one percent more will mean. The same applies to stock benefits, executive deferred compensation plans, everything.

Here are a few tips to negotiate a better compensation package.

Determine your "walk away". This first step is by far the most valuable. Your walkaway is the number, which based on your objective research is the lowest amount can accept while still feeling valued. The key here is to frame your walk away in this manner:

"At what number do I feel as if I am being taken advantage of, and not being paid what I am truly worth?"

This is your walkaway, the salary amount at which you will be prepared to support your position and if this number is not met, you will walk away.

Here's how:

Salary information websites such as salary.com, glassdoor.com and indeed.com will list comparable salaries for the role in question.

What these sites do not do however is factor in your specific experience. If you bring more to the table than what is required for the role, you should receive a package commensurate with that experience, and more importantly a package which reflects how your unique contribution will benefit the company. Remember your "so what". This is where it will have the greatest impact.

Entering the negotiation knowing what you will and will not accept provides the foundation for you to really talk and also listen. You will worry less about figuring out the math on the fly because you already have your game plan.

This approach worked recently for my friend Kristen, as part of her annual review. The company was handing out 2% salary increases and based on her results from the prior year, she felt she deserved more. She asked around and learned what others in her field were making and she knew that employee retention was an important initiative for the company. She lined up these three points and went into the negotiations confident that what she was asking for was fair and reasonable. As a result of her persuasive and polished positioning, she got a meeting with her Vice President and her Human Resource leader to discuss her rationale and talk more about the request. That's a great start.

Rethink your approach. Contrary to popular belief, women are often times more successful than men in negotiations. This happens when women use their inherent mindset and predisposition for collaboration. Successful female negotiators use tactics which come naturally to women rather than try to overcompensate or "act like a man". We are not men, we are women. And when we show up with confidence and knowing our worth, they don't see us coming. They are not prepared, but we are.

Collaborative mindset. Women are more likely to approach a negotiation truly expecting a favorable outcome for all. Rather than "I win, you lose", a female will frame the discussion around what's in it for everyone. An added benefit of reframing here is that you will feel less dread and more optimism in approaching the discussion. The outcome? More confidence. And as we now know, confidence impacts outcomes.

Relational approach. With a relational approach, women go into a negotiation as if negotiating for others. Statements like "we" rather than "I" and advocating for the team rather than the individual are common tactics which yield better results. Women are often more successful when negotiating for others so think about your salary and the impact or benefit to your family, your circle of friends, your parents. Visualize how the additional money in your wallet will change things for the better. This will also boost your advocacy and help to remove the emotion.

Other things to consider:

A compensation package today looks a lot different than it did twenty years ago. I'm not talking about straight salary; I'm referring to the entire package. In some cases, the hiring manager's hands may be tied. While this is not the norm, it does happen. In this situation it's best to have a few suggestions for how else they can help you feel valued. Perks will vary based on the industry and position. I recommend you make a list and think creatively about what else you can ask for and receive in lieu of more dollars.

Salary then... A fixed regular payment, typically paid on a monthly or biweekly basis but often express as an annual sum, made by an employer to an employee, especially a professional or white-collar worker.	• Salary now... • Variable (performance-based upside, commission) • PTO days • Transportation costs • Childcare • Company stock • Early review • Dry cleaning • Overtime • Bonus (not performance based) • Benefits (health, profit sharing, fitness, mental health)

Amplify

Money has long been a taboo topic among women and women often don't discuss salary with other women. Fortunately, in recent years this has changed for the better and many women are including the topic of salary in their discussions with each other. In fact, Brooke Baldwin, former CNN anchor advocates for women sharing salary information with other women. And for men sharing this information as well. Money talk can create tension and hard feelings, and Brooke and I both suggest this idea in the spirit of arming your colleagues with the information they need in order to negotiate from a position of knowledge. I'm not suggesting you go out and broadcast your salary, or demand to know what your best friend is earning. I am suggesting however that you start a conversation. You can talk in ranges, generalities, prior positions, ballparks, or anything which provides more data for you to feel confident about your value. Your confidence in cold hard facts will be critical to determine and stand by your walk away number.

Your Call to Action

Take a look at your current salary and do some research on where you fall compared with like positions. Are you happy with those results? Great. Not so happy? Line up your three key points and start working these into your Power Positioning Statement so you are prepared to demonstrate why you deserve more.

Chapter 9
Women cannot have it all

"Imperfect men have been empowered and permitted to run the world since the beginning of time. It's time for imperfect women to grant themselves permission to join them. Perfection is not a prerequisite of leadership."
-Abby Wambach

Ah, the elusive unicorn.
The dream. The holy grail. What all women strive for.
Work + Life = Balance

I've facilitated hundreds of workshops in four different continents, and I've led large global teams. I teach at Boston University, and I've been on close to fifty expert panels. In every country and in every city, in every ballroom, classroom or zoom meeting, without fail the same question always comes up.

"How do you manage work life balance?"

I'll never forget the stunned hush which fell over the room when I answered this question in front of 500 people in San Antonio, Texas several years ago. I was the lunch speaker at a Marriott event and the last question posed to me was the infamous...

"How do you manage work life balance?" My response was simple and not immediately well received.

"I don't," I answered. "Work/life balance is a myth only asked of women, and we need to stop asking about it and striving for this unattainable goal".

It was absolutely scandalous! There was an audible and communal gasp of disbelief. Mouths gaped open.

I tried to soften this with my follow up comment:

"And anyone who tells you they are successfully managing the competing demands of family, work, and self-care is either lying to you or kidding themselves."

This did not really soften the blow.

Fast forward to today and I still stand by my answer, now more than ever.

The image of the uber-mom, rolling up to soccer practice in her SUV, looking not only presentable but professional with a gym-fit body, running a meeting on her phone with her wireless earbuds while handing sliced oranges and water bottles out the car window, groceries in the back seat, skillfully managing multiple children and deadlines - hers and everyone's, dinner, travel schedules, neighbors, the household and late-night emails - has got to go.

How is mastering all of this balance?

It is not.

I need a nap from just writing this description. To prove my point, let's start with those who supposedly do "Have It All." I choose Beyoncé as a prime example.

She's a powerhouse. She's her own brand. She's one of the highest paid singers in the world right now and she's the gold standard of success for what many women aspire to be. There are even mugs espousing how many hours in the day Beyoncé has, and that you do as well so…

GET IT ALL DONE!

What many people forget (or don't know in the first place) is that she also has a team. A massive team. Beyoncé's company has an estimated 200 employees.

Her personal staff includes a hair stylist making over $1,000,000 per year and a business manager also reported to be making in the seven figures.

And let's talk about her systems which make her life easier.
Her monthly expenses are in the millions.
She reportedly spends $500,000 per month on rent for her vacation home, $75,000 on jet rentals and fuel, $7,500 a month on a live-in chef, $10,000 for her publicist, $8,000 for a bodyguard, $4,000 on a dietitian, $7,000 for her personal trainer, and $4,000 on her maid.

All to be the Unicorn, to live the legend.

I say, good for her. She earned it and she deserves it. Now let's bring this back to you and me and real life. Or what I like to call the: "There is no way I can do this alone so stop telling me I can" proclamation.

Beyoncé is an extreme example so let's take a look at Jane Fraser, the CEO of Citigroup. Jane made a splash in 2020 as the first female CEO of a big bank. As it should be. This was huge for women everywhere. Shortly after she was named CEO, there were a series of news articles talking about her success and what it took for her to get to the top.

When asked about her "work/life balance", she responded with answers like," it was the toughest thing I had to do" and that she felt "exhausted" and "guilty".

Really? Is this how we want to live our lives? I don't hear anything about balance there – do you? Again, I ask, how is this balance to anyone?

While we're at it, are any male CEOs out there on record as saying they're "exhausted" and "guilty"? Nope.

Not one. I checked.

Men are unapologetically imbalanced in other areas of their lives because they have prioritized career success.

Fraser is also quoted as saying she has the support of a great partner, and everyone would agree this is key. What about the women who don't have a great partner? What if their partner isn't so great? What if their partner is working, too - unlike Mr. Fraser who left his job to run the family?

Or...brace yourself here, what if the female executive doesn't have a partner at all?

Then what? Who helps? The village? The nanny? Her mother? The Unicorn?

Jane certainly needs and wisely chooses to get help (or, pays for help because she can afford to pay for help with the salary that comes with her CEO position) so there's strike two for the illusion of work/life balance. What about the other 98%?
How is a working mother, up and coming college graduate or senior level executive with teenagers at home supposed to achieve it all?

Simple. Stop trying.

Focus on what you DO have. You now have the knowledge that work/life balance does not exist and you have the opportunity to make specific choices and tradeoffs. Strategic decisions that you can make with your family, your partner or with yourself. The key here is understanding that these are choices, and the knowledge to make these choices unapologetically. Just like men.

And can we all stop saying "you have as many hours in the day as Beyoncé"? Because you do not.

Your Call to Action:

Your CTA here depends on where you are now and where you want to go.

If you are just starting out in your career, make the conscious decision now to draw clear boundaries relating to your work and personal life, and stick to them. This works and is proven to be effective in developing successful leaders. The happier and more productive you are in your personal life, the happier and more productive you will be at work.

Write down one, just one work/life balance boundary which you will defend ruthlessly. Write in down and list it in your confidence manifesto which you can find here: **https://nancymedoff.com/unmute**

If you're a senior leader, this is your opportunity to lead by example. Check your own expectations and forsake expediency for harmony. Simply recognizing that your life choices are not other people's life choices is a very big first step. I've worked for more than one lunatic boss who had no boundaries and no interest in ensuring those on her team led happy, fulfilled lives. And you know what? They didn't. They were constantly stressed out and ran around frenetically trying to get it all done.

If you are a maniacal boss and have no balance, do not impose your work style on the people who work for you. You will end up creating a bunch of "mini-yous" who are also miserable and so goes the cycle.

Instead, allow the women on your team some grace. Look back on your journey and where your struggles were. Then look for opportunities to provide guidance and support in these areas for those you mentor or lead. As you look back, choose one thing you could have done differently and provide the resources and space for your team to experience this differently. How rewarding would it be to see an area which was a struggle for you become a core value for the team?

The Confidence Manifesto

If you've made it this far, you're committed to nine Calls to Action which you will focus on to Speak Up and Stand Out. Here we pull these actions together in your own Confidence Manifesto and in doing so, walk the talk.

Confidence is a skill and yes, like any other skill you can actively work on improving, increasing and mastering this skill. I can tell you from experience, this works. I've seen the women I work with make commitments to themselves, practice these behaviors daily and in my client Kristen's words, "gain the confidence needed to finally exhale".

I'll give you a real life, personal example. Me. After a successful keynote speech where I train women how to advocate for themselves, people often ask me: Were you always this way? This outgoing? This confident?
The answer is no, and I'd love to tell you how that changed. My story is about a little girl who won the Screwy Screamer award at Camp Chickami in 1976 and thus became an advocate for women to speak up.

When I was a seven, I was a crazy and wild kid. I mean a total in-your-face extrovert. Always talking, always laughing, sometimes causing trouble and super outgoing. One day at Camp Chickami, located outside of Boston, I was awarded the "Screwy Screamer" award. This was a great honor at Camp Chickami and a highly coveted award. This award goes to the screwiest, loudest, most fun, and generally craziest kid at camp.

In short, it's a big deal.

When presented with this award, I promptly broke down and cried. But these were not tears of joy. I was sobbing in front of the whole camp and I was very, very upset because I didn't understand what was happening. All I could see was people laughing and pointing at me. Everyone.

Here's where it gets interesting.

When I turned around, my older sister Laura was right beside me, bending down on her knees so she was eye level to me. She was hugging me and telling me that everything was ok and that the award was in fact a good thing.

She explained to me this award meant that people were happy for me, liked who I was and wanted to hear what I had to say. They were not, in fact making fun of me, they were celebrating me. Think about that. My assumption was that they were laughing at me, when in reality they were applauding and supporting me. How many times have you assumed that people aren't interested in what you have to say? Often times when we feel safe and comfortable, when we are in our natural habitat, we can freely be who we are. We are confident, authentic and our real selves. It's the times when we are in unfamiliar territory, when we are vulnerable, that we lack the confidence to speak up for ourselves, and for others.

My sister repeatedly stuck up for me when we were kids (I'm looking at you, bully Bruce Gorski) and in doing so gave me the greatest gift ever – my voice. She taught me to speak up, to stick up for myself, and to unapologetically step into who I really am. In essence, she taught me to be confident. She then lived her life as an introvert, quietly doing her thing in the background, supporting everyone she loves.

What I learned that day on the grass at Camp Chickami, and then forced myself to practice for decades, helped me transform from a shaking, scared little girl into a confident, strong woman and global keynote speaker.

My purpose is helping people, specifically women, to truly believe they are worthy of being heard. Then giving them the tools so they can speak up to stand out. Like my big sister did for me.

What exactly is a Confidence Manifesto, you ask? It's a written proclamation by you, to you and for you,

declaring your intentions to implement your ideas and plan of action. Remember the Calls to Action at the end of each chapter? Here you can list these micro steps in one place to start off each day with a plan of action. You can find it here:
www.nancymedoff.com/unmute

I live every day to empower women of all ages and backgrounds, and I won't stop until women everywhere have the tools to step into their authenticity, recognize their own power, know their worth and earn a seat at the table.

Then build a bigger table.

If not now, when?

Acknowledgements

My tribe. You know who you are. In fact, you're probably nodding as you're reading this. You know how grateful I am for you because I tell you often, but not often enough. So let me say it again. Thank you. I am grateful for your support and the laughs, the heated discussions, the commiseration, the very, very early morning phone calls, the evening virtual wine dates around the globe, the "hang on I'm just going through TSA" s, the girl's get-a-aways, all of it. Thank you. From the bottom of my heart.

My family. Loud, crazy and the reason I grew up feisty. In my house with four kids and constant chaos, you spoke up or you weren't heard. It was survival of the fittest from getting your slice of pizza to making sure you didn't get pummeled when we played full contact games in the pitch-black basement. I'd walk in front of a bus for each one of you.

My Love. Without a doubt, the person for whom I am most grateful is my husband, Danny. I hesitated to "thank my husband" in a book which is all about women's empowerment. Cringe. Throughout my career in corporate sales, I often thought how much easier my life would be if I had a partner. Easier to travel the world, easier to buy my first home, easier to face health crises, you name it. I wore my single status as a badge of honor. I was successful, independent and needed no-one. I made my way in the world on my own and was proud of it. I remember Sheryl Sandberg getting railed back in the day because she had a support system to help her "Lean In". Women everywhere judged her and called her soft because she espoused how choosing the right partner made such a difference. I was one of those women.

I get it now. Life isn't easier with Danny by my side but it's sure a hell of a lot better. And for you, love of my life, I am eternally grateful.

"If you're offered a ride on a rocket ship, you don't ask what seat. Just get on."
-Sheryl Sandberg

Resources & Sources

www.nancymedoff.com/unmute

Books which changed my life:
- The Confidence Code
    Katy Kay and Claire Shipman
- Lean In: Women, Work, and the Will to Lead
    Sheryl Sandberg
- Presence: Bringing Your Boldest Self to Your Biggest Challenges
    Amy Cuddy

Ted Talks worth seeing:
- Why we have too few woman leaders by Sheryl Sandberg
    - https://www.ted.com/talks/sheryl_sandberg_why_we_have_too_few_women_leaders?language=en
- Your body language may shape who you are by Amy Cuddy
    - https://www.youtube.com/watch?v=Ks-_Mh1QhMc&t=5s
- The power of vulnerability by Brené Brown
    - https://www.youtube.com/watch?v=iCvmsMzlF7o

Articles I reference in the book:
- https://www.kornferry.com/insights/articles/women-ceo-insights
- https://www.youtube.com/watch?v=zbm6brTA1BI
- https://www.nytimes.com/2019/11/20/us/politics/women-voices-authority.html
- https://www.frac.tl/work/marketing-research/publisher-survey/

- https://journals.sagepub.com/doi/abs/10.1177/0361684312455524

Made in the USA
Columbia, SC
08 May 2022